GOD'S LITTLE INSTRUCTION BOOK FOR WOMEN

Honor Books
Tulsa, Oklahoma

God's Little Instruction Book for Women
ISBN 1-56292-862-7
Copyright © 2000 by Honor Books
P. O. Box 55388
Tulsa, Oklahoma 74155

Manuscript prepared by W. B. Freeman Concepts, Tulsa, Oklahoma

Introduction

God's Little Instruction Book for Women is a collection of dynamic quotes and sayings, spanning the wisdom of the centuries. Each quote is accompanied by a scripture that provides spiritual perspective. Together, these two elements offer comfort, guidance, hope, and encouragement—and even a laugh or two.

This little book was designed to be fun reading, yet thought-provoking. It will challenge you to expand your outlook and fulfill your potential as a woman. Whether you work within or beyond the home—or both—these timeless thoughts will recharge your inner being and give you sound advice as a bonus. Enjoy your time absorbing the wisdom and hope in these words—words carefully chosen with you in mind.

My job is to take care of the possible
and trust God with the impossible.

And they that know thy name will put their trust in thee:
for thou, LORD, hast not forsaken them that seek thee.

PSALM 9:10

*W*hen Mother Teresa received her Nobel Prize, she was asked, "What can we do to promote world peace?" She replied, "Go home and love your family."

Let love and faithfulness never leave you; bind them around your neck, write them on the tablet of your heart.

PROVERBS 3:3 NIV

You are never so high as when
you are on your knees.

Humble yourselves in the sight of the Lord, and he shall lift you up.

JAMES 4:10

*G*ive your troubles to God: He will
be up all night anyway.

He will not allow your foot to slip; He who keeps you will not slumber.

PSALM 121:3 NASB

We should seize every opportunity to give encouragement. Encouragement is oxygen to the soul.

A man hath joy by the answer of his mouth: and a word spoken in due season, how good is it!

PROVERBS 15:23

𝒴ou may give without loving, but you cannot love without giving.

For God so loved the world, that he gave his only begotten Son, that whosoever believeth in him should not perish, but have everlasting life.

JOHN 3:16

When I come to the end of my rope,
God is there to take over.

He hath said, I will never leave thee, nor forsake thee.

HEBREWS 13:5

*T*he Lord can do great things through those who don't care who gets the credit.

A man's pride shall bring him low: But honour shall uphold the humble in spirit.

PROVERBS 29:23

*W*hat sunshine is to flowers, smiles are to humanity. They are but trifles, to be sure, but scattered along life's pathway, the good they do is inconceivable.

A happy heart makes the face cheerful.

PROVERBS 15:13 NIV

I regret often that I have spoken; never that I have been silent.

In the multitude of words there wanteth not sin: but he that refraineth his lips is wise.

PROVERBS 10:19

"*I* can forgive, but I cannot forget" is only another way of saying, "I will not forgive." Forgiveness ought to be like a canceled note—torn in two, and burned up, so that it never can be shown against one.

And be ye kind one to another, tenderhearted, forgiving one another,
even as God for Christ's sake hath forgiven you.

EPHESIANS 4:32

*W*orry is like a rocking chair:
It gives you something to do,
but doesn't get you anywhere.

Casting the whole of your care [all your anxieties, all your worries, all your concerns, once and for all] on Him, for He cares for you affectionately and cares about you watchfully.

1 PETER 5:7 AMP

*L*ook around you and be distressed,
Look within you and be depressed, Look
to Jesus and be at rest.

In my distress I cried unto the Lord, and he heard me.

PSALM 120:1

There is no greater love than the love that holds on where there seems nothing left to hold on to.

Love never fails [never fades out or becomes obsolete or comes to an end].

1 CORINTHIANS 13:8 AMP

*D*aily prayers will diminish your cares.

Evening, and morning, and at noon, will I pray,
and cry aloud: and he shall hear my voice.

PSALM 55:17

*B*e like a postage stamp—stick to one thing till you get there.

Be steadfast, immovable, always abounding in the work of the Lord, knowing that your toil is not in vain in the Lord.

1 CORINTHIANS 15:58   NASB

 good laugh is sunshine in a house.

The light in the eyes [of him whose heart is joyful] rejoices the hearts of others.

PROVERBS 15:30 AMP

*E*ach loving act says loud and clear,
"I love you. God loves you.
I care. God cares."

*Beloved, let us love one another: for love is of God; and every one
that loveth is born of God . . . for God is love.*

1 JOHN 4:7-8

I have held many things in my hands
and lost them all; but the things
I have placed in God's hands,
those I always possess.

I know whom I have believed, and am persuaded that he is able to keep
that which I have committed unto him against that day.

2 TIMOTHY 1:12

A good deed is never lost; he who sows courtesy reaps friendship, and he who plants kindness gathers love.

Whatsoever a man soweth, that shall he also reap. And let us not be weary in well doing: for in due season we shall reap, if we faint not.

GALATIANS 6:7,9

*K*ind words can be short and easy to speak, but their echoes are truly endless.

She opens her mouth with skillful and godly Wisdom, and on her tongue is the law of kindness [giving counsel and instruction].

PROVERBS 31:26 AMP

*N*othing beats love at first sight except love with insight.

The beginning of wisdom is this: Get wisdom,
and whatever else you get, get insight.

PROVERBS 4:7 NRSV

A house is made of walls and beams;
a home is made of love and dreams.

Better a meal of vegetables where there is love than a fattened calf with hatred.

PROVERBS 15:17 NIV

The best way to hold a man is in your arms.

The man should give his wife all that is her right as a married woman,
and the wife should do the same for her husband.

1 CORINTHIANS 7:3 TLB

*N*inety percent of the friction of daily life is caused by the wrong tone of voice.

A man finds joy in giving an apt reply—and how good is a timely word!

PROVERBS 15:23 NIV

*F*orgiveness is giving love when there is no reason to.

Blessed are the merciful, for they shall obtain mercy.

MATTHEW 5:7 NKJV

*N*othing is so strong as gentleness.
Nothing is so gentle as real strength.

Thou hast also given me the shield of Thy salvation, And Thy right
hand upholds me; and Thy gentleness makes me great.

PSALM 18:35 NASB

*E*veryone has patience. Successful
people learn to use it.

*But let patience have her perfect work, that ye may be
perfect and entire, wanting nothing.*

JAMES 1:4

*W*atch out for temptation—the more you see of it the better it looks.

Keep watching and praying, that you may not come into temptation.

MARK 14:38 NASB

It is such a comfort to drop the
tangles of life into God's hands
and leave them there.

Cast your cares on the LORD and he will sustain you.

PSALM 55:22 NIV

*F*riendship improves happiness, and abates misery, by doubling our joy, and dividing our grief.

A friend loves at all times, and a brother is born for adversity.

PROVERBS 17:17 NIV

Everyone has an invisible sign hanging from his neck saying, "Make me feel important!"

Therefore encourage one another and build each other up, just as in fact you are doing.

1 THESSALONIANS 5:11 NIV

You cannot do a kindness too soon,
because you never know how soon
it will be too late!

But encourage one another day after day, as long as it is still called "Today."

HEBREWS 3:13 NASB

*S*tack every bit of criticism
between two layers of praise.

Correct, rebuke and encourage—with great patience and careful instruction.

2 TIMOTHY 4:2 NIV

*I*n trying times, don't quit trying.

And let us not grow weary in well-doing, for in due season
we shall reap, if we do not lose heart.

GALATIANS 6:9 RSV

*T*o love what you do and feel
that it matters—how could
anything else be more fun?

When you eat the labor of your hands, you shall be happy, and it shall be well with you.

PSALM 128:2 NKJV

*L*ife is a coin. You can spend it
any way you wish, but you
can only spend it once.

For what is your life? It is even a vapor that appears
for a little time and then vanishes away.

JAMES 4:14 NKJV

$\mathcal{D}$iligence is the mother of good fortune.

The hand of the diligent makes one rich.

PROVERBS 10:4 NKJV

The most wasted of all days is that on which one has not laughed.

A happy heart makes the face cheerful, but heartache crushes the spirit.

PROVERBS 15:13 NIV

You can accomplish more in one hour
with God than one lifetime without Him.

Walk in wisdom . . . redeeming the time.

COLOSSIANS 4:5

*C*ourage is resistance to fear, mastery
of fear—not the absence of fear.

Therefore, take up the full armor of God, that you may be able to resist in the
evil day, and having done everything, to stand firm. Stand firm therefore.

EPHESIANS 6:13-14 NASB

The art of being wise is the art of knowing what to overlook.

A man's wisdom gives him patience; it is to his glory to overlook an offense.

PROVERBS 19:11 NIV

Triumph is just "umph" added to try.

And let us not be weary in well doing: for in due season
we shall reap, if we faint not.

GALATIANS 6:9

*P*eople don't care how much you know, until they know how much you care . . . about them.

And though I have the gift of prophecy, and understand all mysteries, and all knowledge; and though I have all faith, so that I could remove mountains, and have not charity, I am nothing.

1 CORINTHIANS 13:2

Good words are worth much, and cost little.

Pleasant words are a honeycomb, sweet to the soul and healing to the bones.

PROVERBS 16:24 NASB

I don't know the secret to success
but the key to failure is to try
to please everyone.

No one can serve two masters; for either he will hate the one and love
the other, or he will hold to one and despise the other.

MATTHEW 6:24 NASB

*N*o one is useless in this world who lightens the burden of it to anyone else.

Bear ye one another's burdens, and so fulfil the law of Christ.

GALATIANS 6:2

*D*o not follow where the path may
lead—go instead where there is
no path and leave a trail.

Your ears shall hear a word behind you, saying, "This is the way, walk in it."

ISAIAH 30:21 NKJV

There is one thing alone that stands the brunt of life throughout its length: a quiet conscience.

If our hearts do not condemn us, we have confidence before God.

1 JOHN 3:21 NIV

My obligation is to do the right thing. The rest is in God's hands.

If you know that he is righteous, you may be sure that everyone who does right is born of him.

1 JOHN 2:29 RSV

*E*xpect great things from God.
Attempt great things for God.

Truly, truly, I say to you, he who believes in Me, the works that I do shall he do also; and greater works than these shall he do; because I go to the Father.

JOHN 14:12 NASB

*D*ost thou love life? Then do not squander time, for that is the stuff life is made of.

Remember how short my time is.

PSALM 89:47

*T*he grass may be greener on the other side, but it still has to be mowed.

Be content with such things as ye have.

HEBREWS 13:5

*E*very job is a self-portrait of the person who does it. Autograph your work with excellence.

Many daughters have done well, But you excel them all.

PROVERBS 31:29 NKJV

*T*he greatest achievements
are those that benefit others.

To be the greatest, be a servant.

MATTHEW 23:11 TLB

*I*f a task is once begun, never leave it
'til it's done. Be the labor great
or small, do it well or not at all.

Whatever your hand finds to do, do it with your might.

ECCLESIASTES 9:10 NKJV

I would rather walk with God in the dark than go alone in the light.

Even when walking through the dark valley of death I will not be afraid,
for you are close beside me, guarding, guiding all the way.

PSALM 23:4 TLB

*A*ll our dreams can come true—if we have the courage to pursue them.

Be strong and courageous, and act; do not fear nor be dismayed,
for the LORD God, my God, is with you.

1 CHRONICLES 28:20 NASB

Remember the banana—when it left the bunch, it got skinned.

Not forsaking the assembling of ourselves together, as the manner of some is; but exhorting one another: and so much the more, as ye see the day approaching.

HEBREWS 10:25

Decisions can take you out of God's will but never out of His reach.

If we are faithless, he will remain faithful, for he cannot disown himself.

2 TIMOTHY 2:13 NIV

"*No*" is one of the few words that can never be misunderstood.

But let your statement be "Yes, yes" or "No, no."

MATTHEW 5:37 NASB

Some people complain because God put thorns on roses, while others praise Him for putting roses among thorns.

Finally, brethren, whatsoever things are true, whatsoever things are honest, whatsoever things are just, whatsoever things are pure, whatsoever things are lovely, whatsoever things are of good report; if there be any virtue, and if there be any praise, think on these things.

PHILIPPIANS 4:8

The bridge you burn now may be the one you later have to cross.

If it be possible, as much as lieth in you, live peaceably with all men.

ROMANS 12:18

*R*eal friends are those who, when you've made a fool of yourself, don't feel you've done a permanent job.

Love . . . bears all things, believes all things, hopes all things, endures all things. Love never fails.

1 CORINTHIANS 13:4,7-8 NKJV

*M*ost people wish to serve God—
but only in an advisory capacity.

*Humble yourselves therefore under the mighty hand of God,
that he may exalt you in due time.*

1 PETER 5:6

*C*onscience is God's built-in warning system. Be very happy when it hurts you. Be very worried when it doesn't.

And herein do I exercise myself, to have always a conscience void of offense toward God, and toward men.

ACTS 24:16

If you don't stand for something you'll fall for anything!

For ye are bought with a price: therefore glorify God in your body,
and in your spirit, which are God's.

1 CORINTHIANS 6:20

*Y*ou should never let adversity get you down—except on your knees.

For I am persuaded, that neither death, nor life, nor angels, nor principalities, nor powers, nor things present, nor things to come . . . shall be able to separate us from the love of God, which is in Christ Jesus our Lord.

ROMANS 8:38-39

The best bridge between hope and despair is often a good night's sleep.

It is vain for you to rise up early, to sit up late, to eat the bread of sorrows: for so he giveth his beloved sleep.

PSALM 127:2

It is good to remember that the teakettle, although up to its neck in hot water, continues to sing.

Rejoice evermore. In every thing give thanks: for this is the will of God in Christ Jesus concerning you.

1 THESSALONIANS 5:16,18

*I*t's good to be a Christian and know it, but it's better to be a Christian and show it!

By this shall all men know that ye are my disciples,
if ye have love one to another.

JOHN 13:35

Sorrow looks back. Worry looks around. Faith looks up.

Fixing our eyes on Jesus, the author and perfecter of faith, who for the joy set before Him endured the cross, despising the shame, and has sat down at the right hand of the throne of God.

HEBREWS 12:2 NASB

*S*ometimes we are so busy adding
up our troubles that we forget
to count our blessings.

I will remember the works of the LORD: surely I will remember thy wonders of
old. I will meditate also of all thy work, and talk of thy doings.

PSALM 77:11-12

$\mathcal{G}$od can heal a broken heart,
but He has to have all the pieces.

My son, give me thine heart.

PROVERBS 23:26

$\mathscr{B}$e more concerned with what God thinks about you than what people think about you.

But seek first the kingdom of God and His righteousness,
and all these things shall be added to you.

MATTHEW 6:33 NKJV

The best way to get the last word is to apologize.

If you have been trapped by what you said, ensnared by the words of your mouth, then do this, my son, to free yourself, since you have fallen into your neighbor's hands: Go and humble yourself; press your plea with your neighbor!

PROVERBS 6:2-3 NIV

*F*orget yourself for others and others will not forget you!

Therefore all things whatsoever ye would that men should do to you, do ye even so to them: for this is the law and the prophets.

MATTHEW 7:12

*T*he secret of contentment is the realization that life is a gift not a right.

But godliness with contentment is great gain. For we brought nothing into this world, and it is certain we can carry nothing out.

1 TIMOTHY 6:6-7

*T*hose who bring sunshine to the lives of others cannot keep it from themselves.

Be not deceived; God is not mocked: for whatsoever a man soweth, that shall he also reap.

GALATIANS 6:7

*I*t's the little things in life that determine the big things.

Thou hast been faithful over a few things, I will make thee ruler over many things: enter thou into the joy of thy lord.

MATTHEW 25:21

Contentment isn't getting what
we want but being satisfied
with what we have.

*Not that I speak in respect of want: for I have learned,
in whatsoever state I am, therewith to be content.*

PHILIPPIANS 4:11

$\mathcal{G}$od plus one is always a majority!

If God be for us, who can be against us?

ROMANS 8:31

Whoever gossips to you will be a gossip of you.

A talebearer revealeth secrets: but he that is of a faithful spirit concealeth the matter.

PROVERBS 11:13

*J*esus is a friend who knows all your faults and still loves you anyway.

But God commendeth his love toward us, in that,
while we were yet sinners, Christ died for us.

ROMANS 5:8

*E*very person should have a special cemetery lot in which to bury the faults of friends and loved ones.

And be ye kind one to another, tenderhearted, forgiving one another,
even as God for Christ's sake hath forgiven you.

EPHESIANS 4:32

A minute of thought is worth
more than an hour of talk.

Set a watch, O LORD, before my mouth; keep the door of my lips.

PSALM 141:3

You can win more friends with your ears than with your mouth.

Let every man be swift to hear, slow to speak, slow to wrath.

JAMES 1:19

*I*t's not the outlook but the
uplook that counts.

Looking unto Jesus the author and finisher of our faith.

HEBREWS 12:2

*I*t isn't hard to make a mountain out of a molehill. Just add a little dirt.

Starting a quarrel is like breaching a dam; so drop the matter before a dispute breaks out.

PROVERBS 17:14 NIV

The art of being a good guest is knowing when to leave.

Withdraw thy foot from thy neighbour's house;
lest he be weary of thee, and so hate thee.

PROVERBS 25:17

*J*esus is a friend who walks in when the world has walked out.

These things I have spoken unto you, that in me ye might have peace. In the world ye shall have tribulation: but be of good cheer; I have overcome the world.

JOHN 16:33

*T*hose who deserve love the least
need it the most.

But I say unto you, Love your enemies, bless them that curse you,
do good to them that hate you, and pray for them which
despitefully use you, and persecute you.

MATTHEW 5:44

$\mathcal{F}$aith is daring the soul to go
beyond what the eyes can see.

For we walk by faith, not by sight.

2 CORINTHIANS 5:7

A critical spirit is like poison ivy—
it only takes a little contact
to spread its poison.

But avoid worldly and empty chatter, for it will lead to further ungodliness.

2 TIMOTHY 2:16 NASB

*T*wo things are hard on the heart—
running up stairs and
running down people.

*Let no corrupt communication proceed out of your mouth, but that which is good
to the use of edifying, that it may minister grace unto the hearers.*

EPHESIANS 4:29

*H*umor is to life what shock absorbers are to automobiles.

Then our mouth was filled with laughter, And our tongue with singing. Then they said among the nations, "The LORD has done great things for them."

PSALM 126:2 NKJV

*K*indness is the oil that takes
the friction out of life.

But the fruit of the Spirit is . . . kindness.

GALATIANS 5:22 NIV

*O*ur days are identical suitcases—all the same size—but some people can pack more into them than others.

Be very careful, then, how you live—not as unwise but as wise, making the most of every opportunity.

EPHESIANS 5:15-16 NIV

To forgive is to set a prisoner free and discover the prisoner was YOU.

For if ye forgive men their trespasses, your heavenly Father will also forgive you: But if ye forgive not men their trespasses, neither will your Father forgive your trespasses.

MATTHEW 6:14-15

The heart is the happiest when
it beats for others.

Greater love hath no man than this, that a man
lay down his life for his friends.

JOHN 15:13

A true friend never gets in your way unless you happen to be going down.

A friend loves at all times, And a brother is born for adversity.

PROVERBS 17:17 NASB

*L*aughter is the brush that sweeps
away the cobwebs of the heart.

*A happy heart is a good medicine and a cheerful mind works
healing, but a broken spirit dries up the bones.*

PROVERBS 17:22 AMP

*G*od has a history of using the
insignificant to accomplish
the impossible.

And Jesus looking upon them saith, With men it is impossible,
but not with God: for with God all things are possible.

MARK 10:27

*P*eople may doubt what you say, but they will always believe what you do.

The tree is known and recognized and judged by its fruit.

MATTHEW 12:33 AMP

*K*indness is a language which the deaf can hear and the blind can see.

For his merciful kindness is great toward us: and the truth of the LORD endureth for ever. Praise ye the LORD.

PSALM 117:2

I make it a rule of Christian duty never to go to a place where there is not room for my Master as well as myself.

Don't be teamed with those who do not love the Lord. . . . How can a
Christian be a partner with one who doesn't believe?

2 CORINTHIANS 6:14-15 TLB

Jesus can turn water into wine, but He can't turn your whining into anything.

Do all things without murmurings and disputings.

PHILIPPIANS 2:14

*T*he smallest deed is better than
the greatest intention!

Let us not love [merely] in theory or in speech but in deed
and in truth (in practice and in sincerity).

1 JOHN 3:18 AMP

I've suffered a great many catastrophes in my life. Most of them never happened.

For God hath not given us the spirit of fear; but of power,
and of love, and of a sound mind.

2 TIMOTHY 1:7

*G*uilt is concerned with the past.
Worry is concerned about the future.
Contentment enjoys the present.

Not that I am implying that I was in any personal want, for I have learned
how to be content (satisfied to the point where I am not
disturbed or disquieted) in whatever state I am.

PHILIPPIANS 4:11 AMP

People with tact have less to retract.

The heart of the righteous weighs its answers,
but the mouth of the wicked gushes evil.

PROVERBS 15:28 NIV

*B*eing at peace with yourself is a direct result of finding peace with God.

And the peace of God, which passeth all understanding,
shall keep your hearts and minds through Christ Jesus.

PHILIPPIANS 4:7

*I*f you want to make an easy job seem mighty hard, just keep putting off doing it.

How long are ye slack to go to possess the land, which the LORD God of your fathers hath given you?

JOSHUA 18:3

*L*ove sees through a telescope
not a microscope.

*Love endures long and is patient and kind . . . it takes no account of the evil
done to it [it pays no attention to a suffered wrong].*

1 CORINTHIANS 13:4-5 AMP

$\mathcal{L}$ife is not a problem to be solved,
but a gift to be enjoyed.

This is the day the LORD has made; let us rejoice and be glad in it.

PSALM 118:24 NIV

A pint of example is worth a barrel full of advice.

Brethren, join in following my example, and observe those who walk according to the pattern you have in us.

PHILIPPIANS 3:17 NASB

*B*eware lest your footprints on the sand of time leave only the marks of a heel.

The memory of the righteous will be a blessing,
but the name of the wicked will rot.

PROVERBS 10:7 NIV

*I*f you were given a nickname
descriptive of your character,
would you be proud of it?

A good name is rather to be chosen than great riches.

PROVERBS 22:1

*I*t's easy to identify people who can't count to ten. They're in front of you in the supermarket express lane.

Be patient with everyone.

1 THESSALONIANS 5:14 NIV

*T*act is the art of making a point
without making an enemy.

Reckless words pierce like a sword, but the tongue of the wise brings healing.

PROVERBS 12:18 NIV

*S*ilence is one of the hardest
arguments to refute.

Whoso keepeth his mouth and his tongue keepeth his soul from troubles.

PROVERBS 21:23

The best antique is an old friend.

Your own friend and your father's friend, forsake them not . . . Better is a
neighbor who is near [in spirit] than a brother who is far off [in heart].

PROVERBS 27:10 AMP

If you can't feed a hundred people then just feed one.

As we have therefore opportunity, let us do good unto all men.

GALATIANS 6:10

*T*he trouble with stretching the truth
is that it's apt to snap back.

*A false witness shall not be unpunished, and he
that speaketh lies shall not escape.*

PROVERBS 19:5

*B*irthdays are good for you.
Statistics show that the people who have
the most live the longest.

So teach us to number our days, that we may apply our hearts unto wisdom.

PSALM 90:12

*F*aults are thick where love is thin.

And above all things have fervent charity among yourselves:
for charity shall cover the multitude of sins.

1 PETER 4:8

*T*he only way to have a
friend is to be one.

A man that hath friends must shew himself friendly.

PROVERBS 18:24

The world wants your best but
God wants your all.

Thou shall love the Lord thy God with all thy heart,
and with all they soul, and with all thy mind.

MATTHEW 22:37

*H*indsight explains the injury that foresight would have prevented.

Do not forsake wisdom, and she will protect you. . . . When you walk, your steps will not be hampered; when you run, you will not stumble.

PROVERBS 4:6,12 NIV

*D*o not in the darkness of night,
what you'd shun in broad daylight.

The night is far spent, the day is at hand: let us therefore cast off the
works of darkness, and let us put on the armour of light.

ROMANS 13:12

I am defeated, and know it, if I meet any human being from whom I find myself unable to learn anything.

A wise man will hear, and will increase learning; and a man of understanding shall attain unto wise counsels.

PROVERBS 1:5

*H*onesty is the first chapter of
the book of wisdom.

Provide things honest in the sight of all men.

ROMANS 12:17

*G*od always gives His best to those
who leave the choice with Him.

Blessed be the LORD, who daily loadeth us with benefits,
even the God of our salvation.

PSALM 68:19

A lot of people mistake a short
memory for a clear conscience.

And herein do I exercise myself, to have always a conscience
void of offense toward God, and toward men.

ACTS 24:16

*F*aith is not belief without proof,
but trust without reservation.

I know whom I have believed, and am persuaded that he is able to
keep that which I have committed unto him against that day.

2 TIMOTHY 1:12

A day hemmed in prayer is
less likely to unravel.

Pray about everything; tell God your needs and don't forget to thank him for his
answers. If you do this you will experience God's peace. . . . His peace
will keep your thoughts and your hearts quiet and at rest.

PHILIPPIANS 4:6-7 TLB

When you flee temptations don't leave a forwarding address.

Now flee from youthful lusts, and pursue righteousness, faith, love and peace, with those who call on the Lord from a pure heart.

2 TIMOTHY 2:22 NASB

A coincidence is a small miracle
where God prefers to
remain anonymous.

Who can put into words and tell the mighty deeds of the Lord?
Or who can show forth all the praise [that is due Him]?

PSALM 106:2 AMP

*S*ometimes the Lord calms the storm;
sometimes He lets the storm rage
and calms His child.

And the peace of God, which transcends all understanding,
will guard your hearts and your minds in Christ Jesus.

PHILIPPIANS 4:7 NIV

The past should be a springboard not a hammock.

This one thing I do, forgetting those things which are behind,
and reaching forth unto those things which are before.

PHILIPPIANS 3:13

The teacher asked the pupils to tell the meaning of loving-kindness. A little boy jumped up and said, "Well, if I was hungry and someone gave me a piece of bread that would be kindness. But if they put a little jelly on it, that would be loving-kindness."

Bless the LORD, O my soul . . . who crowneth thee with lovingkindness and tender mercies; Who satisfieth thy mouth with good things.

PSALM 103:1,4-5

*L*aughter is a tranquilizer
with no side effects.

A merry heart doeth good like a medicine.

PROVERBS 17:22

*G*od never asks about our ability or our inability—just our availability.

I heard the voice of the LORD, saying, Whom shall I send, and who will go for us? Then said I, Here am I; send me.

ISAIAH 6:8

*W*hether you think you can or think you can't, you're right.

As he thinketh in his heart, so is he.

PROVERBS 23:7

*T*he best way to cheer yourself up
is to cheer up somebody else.

Give, and it shall be given unto you.

LUKE 6:38

Failure isn't falling down. It's staying down.

A just man falleth seven times, and riseth up again.

PROVERBS 24:16

*N*obody can make you feel inferior
without your consent.

I am fearfully and wonderfully made.

PSALM 139:14

You built no great cathedrals
That centuries applaud,
But with a grace exquisite
Your life cathedraled God.

Ye are the temple of the living God; as God
hath said, I will dwell in them, and walk
in them.

2 CORINTHIANS 6:16

The highest pinnacle of the spiritual life is not joy in unbroken sunshine but absolute and undoubting trust in the love of God.

Whatsoever is born of God overcometh the world: and this is the victory that overcometh the world, even our faith.

1 JOHN 5:4

*W*hen home is ruled according to God's Word, angels might be asked to stay with us, and they would not find themselves out of their element.

I will meditate in thy precepts, and have respect unto thy ways.
I will delight myself in thy statutes: I will not forget thy word.

PSALM 119:15-16

References

Unless otherwise indicated, all Scripture quotations are taken from the *King James Version* of the Bible.

Scripture quotations marked NIV are taken from *The Holy Bible, New International Version*®. NIV®. Copyright © 1973, 1978, 1984 by International Bible Society. Used by permission of Zondervan Publishing House. All rights reserved.

Scripture quotations marked NASB are taken from the *New American Standard Bible*. Copyright © The Lockman Foundation 1960, 1962, 1963, 1968, 1971, 1972, 1973, 1975, 1977. Used by permission.

Scripture quotations marked AMP are taken from *The Amplified Bible. Old Testament* copyright © 1965, 1987 by Zondervan Corporation, Grand Rapids, Michigan. *New Testament* copyright © 1958, 1987 by The Lockman Foundation, La Habra, California. Used by permission.

Scripture quotations marked NKJV are taken from *The New King James Version*. Copyright © 1979, 1980, 1982, 1994 by Thomas Nelson, Inc., Publishers. Used by permission.

Verses marked TLB are taken from *The Living Bible*, copyright © 1971. Used by permission of Tyndale House Publishers, Inc., Wheaton, Illinois 60189. All rights reserved.

Scripture quotations marked RSV are taken from *The Revised Standard Version Bible*, copyright © 1946, Old Testament section copyright © 1952 by the Division of Christian Education of the Churches of Christ in the United States of America and is used by permission.

Scripture quotations marked NRSV are taken from *The New Revised Standard Version of the Bible*, copyright © 1989 by the Division of Christian Education of the National Council of the Churches of Christ in the United Sates of America. Used by permission. All rights reserved.

Acknowledgements

Ruth Bell Graham (6), Mother Teresa (7, 26, 128), Jean Hodges (8), George M. Adams (10), Helen Pearson (13), Joseph Addison (14), Cyrus (15), Henry Ward Beecher (16), G. W. C. Thomas (19), Betty Mills (20), Josh Billings (21, 126), Thackeray (22), Joyce Heinrigh and Annette La Placa (23), Joyce Earline Steelburg (24), St. Basil (25), Catherine Graham (41), Lillian Dickson (42), Cervantes (43), Sebastian-Roche (44), Mark Twain (46, 110, 114), William James (47), Zig Ziglar (49), William Feather (50), Bill Cosby (51), Charles Dickens (52), Euripedes (54), Martin Luther King Jr. (55), William Carey (56), Benjamin Franklin (57), Dennis Waitley (60), Mary Gardner Brainard (62), Walt Disney (63), Arnold H. Glasgow (106), Mort Walker (107), Richard Exley (108), John Newton (111), Mark Steele (112), Olin Miller (117), Joseph P. Dooley (120), June Henderson (124), Dr. John Olson (125), Reverand Larry Lorenzoni (130), James Howell (131), Ralph Waldo Emerson (132), Charles H. Spurgeon (135, 155), George Herbert Palmer (136), Thomas Jefferson (137), Jim Elliot (138), Doug Larsen (139), Elton Trueblood (140), Ivern Ball (145), Merceline Cox (147), Henry Ford (149), Mary Pickford (151), Eleanor Roosevelt (152), Thomas Fessenden (153), A. W. Thorold (154).

Additional copies of this book and other titles
in the *God's Little Instruction Book* series
are available from your local bookstore.

God's Little Instruction Book, leather edition
God's Little Instruction Book for Mom, leather edition
God's Little Instruction Book for Men, leather edition

If you have enjoyed this book or if it has impacted your life,
we would like to hear from you. Please contact us at:

Honor Books
Department E
P. O. Box 55388
Tulsa, Oklahoma 74155

Or by e-mail at: info@honorbooks.com